The Three

"I am hungry,"
said Father Goat.

"I am hungry,"
said Mother Goat.

"I am hungry,"
said Baby Goat.

3

The three goats went trip *trap* trip *trap* onto the bridge.

5

"Who is that going trip *trap* on my bridge?" called Troll.

"It is us,"
said the three goats.

"Well, I am going
to eat you up,"
said Troll.

"Oh no, you are not!" said Father Goat.

"Oh no, you are not!" said Mother Goat.

"Oh no, you are not!" said Baby Goat.

Troll looked at
the three goats.
He went back under
the bridge.

The three goats went trip *trap* trip *trap* over the bridge.

"I am not hungry now," said Father Goat.

"I am not hungry now," said Mother Goat.

"I am not hungry now," said Baby Goat.